Down on the Farm

FISH

Sally Morgan

QED Publishing

First published in the UK in 2007 by
QED Publishing
A Quarto Group company
226 City Road
London ECIV 2TT
www.qed-publishing.co.uk

A catalogue record for this book is available
from the British Library.

ISBN 978-1-84538-689-4

Written by Sally Morgan
Designed by Tara Frese
Editor Corrine Ochiltree
Picture Researcher Nic Dean
Illustrations by Chris Davidson

Publisher Steve Evans
Creative Director Zeta Davies
Senior Editor Hannah Ray

Printed and bound in China

Picture credits

Key: t = top, b = bottom, c = centre,
l = left, r = right, FC = front cover

Alamy / Jerome Yeats 14, Profimedia International
s.r.o. 18 tl; **Ardea** / John Daniels 6, Keb Lucas 7, John
Swedberg 12, Pat Morris 17 tl; **Barn Goddess
Fainters** / Stephanie Dicke 17 bl; **Corbis** / Carlos
Barria/Reuters title page 1, Clouds Hill Imaging Ltd 8
tl, Suthep Kritsanavarin/epa 19; **Ecoscene** / Robert
Pickett 8 cb, Peter Hulme 10, Reinhard Dirscherl 16 tr;
FLPA / Reinard Dirscher 4, Bill Broadhurst 5, Norbert
Wu/Minden Pictures 9, David Hosking 11, Frank W.
Lane 16 br, Wil Meinderts/Foto Natura 17 br; **Mik
Gates** 13 18 br; NHPA 22.

CONTENTS

Fish on the farm   4

Fish from mouth to tail   6

It's a fish's life...   8

Underwater life   10

Fish for food   12

Eat fish, *be brainy!*   14

Fishy friends   16

Fish around the world   18

A fishy mobile   20

Glossary   22

Index   23

Ideas for teachers and parents   24

Words in **bold** can be found in the Glossary on page 22.

Fish on the farm

Did you know that fish give us meat, oil and even eggs to eat? Fish are animals that live in water. They live in seas, lakes and rivers, all over the world.

This large fish is a carp. Carp live in freshwater lakes and rivers.

Some types of fish such as carp, trout, salmon, sea bass, cod and tilapia are raised in special fish farms. Fish farms can be based at sea or on land. Sea fish farms keep the fish in huge cages in the water. Fish farms on land keep the fish in large ponds.

5

Fish from mouth to tail

Fish have **fins** instead of arms and legs. They use their fins and tail to swim easily through the water. They do not have lungs like us, instead they breathe using **gills**.

Tail

Fins

Eye

Nostrils

Body covered in scales

Flap over gills

Mouth

Fish come in different sizes. An Atlantic salmon from a fish farm can weigh 9kg but most weigh about 4–5kg. That is the same as four or five bags of sugar. These salmon grow up to 1.5m long. Farmed trout are smaller. They can grow up to 75cm and weigh up to 1kg.

This spotty fish is a trout.

Size of a six-year-old child

Size of a salmon

FARM FACT

The world record for the largest Atlantic salmon caught on a fishing rod was 35.89kg. That's about the weight of two six year-olds! It was caught in the Tana River, in Norway. Now that's a big fish!

It's a fish's life...

Trout begin their lives when the female fish lays her eggs. A tiny fish grows inside each egg. After a few weeks, mini fish called **fry** push out of the egg. They hide among plants to avoid being eaten by other fish. After a couple of weeks, the fry start swimming and eating. They eat tiny pieces of food floating in the water.

Fry do not have to eat for the first two weeks of their lives. They are born with a ready-made meal in a special egg sac.

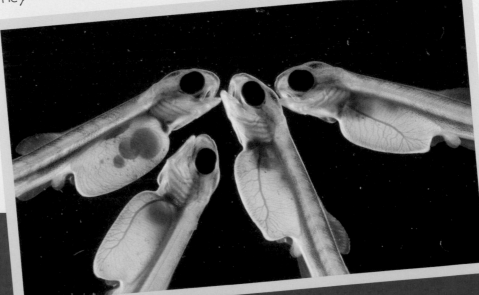

Young fish that live on a fish farm are fed special fish food every day to make them grow quickly. They reach their full size in just nine months. In the wild, it takes two years for a fish to become fully grown.

9

Underwater life

Fish have to be kept in water to stay alive. In fish farms, they are given food that has lots of **nutrients** in it to keep them healthy.

This man is feeding fish in a fish farm.

FARM
FACT
Wild salmon
feed on many
different types
of small fish.

Fish farms on land have different ponds for
the fish to live in. These fish always have
clean, fresh water to swim around in. Clean
water pours into the ponds while the dirty
water is taken away. The fish are moved
from pond to pond, as they get larger.

Fish for food

Millions and millions of fish are eaten by people each year. Most are caught in the wild, but a quarter of all fish that are eaten around the world come from fish farms. This helps to protect wild fish numbers. When the farmed fish are big enough, they are caught in nets and taken to fish markets to be sold.

This man is catching a salmon on a fish farm.

Fish don't really have fingers! The finger shapes are cut from the tasty meat of cod or a fish called a hoki.

Do you like fish fingers or fish and chips? There are lots of different ways of cooking fish. It can be **grilled**, **baked**, fried, and some fish can even be eaten raw.

13

Eat fish, be brainy!

The meat of fish, such as trout and salmon, contains a lot of oil. Fish oil is very good for us because it contains lots of **vitamins**. The oil helps our bodies to stay healthy. It also keeps our bodies bendy because it oils all of our **joints**.

Cod-liver oil comes in little capsules.

This colourful fish is
a rainbow trout.

This spotty, silver
fish is a salmon.

Fish oil also contains something called
omega-3. Omega-3 helps to Keep our heart
healthy and it is also good for our brain.
So, what are you waiting for? Eat up!

Fishy friends

COD

The largest cod ever caught weighed an incredible 96kg. That's the same as five six-year-old children! Cod have a thick, hair-like organ sticking out from the bottom of their chin. This is called a barbel and they use it to taste things.

TILAPIA

Wild tilapia live in rivers and lakes in Africa. They are farmed in Africa and parts of Asia. Wild tilapia females are great mothers. They look after their young by guarding their eggs and caring for the fry when they hatch.

16

HALIBUT

The halibut is a large, flat fish. Imagine a fish that has been squashed completely flat – that's a halibut! Its fins are found along the edge of its body and both its eyes are on the top of its head!

CARP

The carp is a large fish that comes from Asia. It has been grown in fish farms for more than 1000 years. It is a cousin of the koi carp that are kept in garden ponds all around the world.

Fish around the world

GERMANY
In many European countries, such as Germany, it is **traditional** to eat carp on Christmas Eve. The carp is eaten with potato salad.

FRANCE
Around the world, 1 April is celebrated as April Fools' Day. In France, children stick paper fish onto their friends' backs as a joke. A person with a fish on their back is called a 'poisson d'Avril' – an April fish!

18

THAILAND

In Thailand, the giant catfish is thought to be a special fish. Eating its meat is supposed to bring good luck. Each year, fishermen hold a special **ceremony** to ask the river god for permission to catch the fish. Just look at the size of this one!

19

A fishy mobile

Make a colourful fish mobile and hang it in a window. You will need a pencil, ruler, coloured card, scissors, fish pictures, white card, crayons, glitter, sequins and wool.

1 Cut out a circle of card that is 20cm wide. Ask an adult to make 6 small holes around the edge of the card. Add another hole in the middle of the circle.

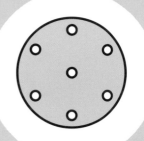

2 Look at the pictures of fish and draw 6 different fish shapes onto card. Ask an adult to cut them out.

3 Ask an adult to make a small hole at the top of each fish. Colour both sides with bright colours and draw on the eyes and mouth. Add sequins or glitter for super-shiny scales.

20

4 Cut 6 pieces of wool, all different lengths between 30cm and 50cm.

5 Tie one end of a length of wool to a fish. Push the other end through one of the holes around the edge of the card circle. Tie a knot in the end of the wool so that it cannot slip back through the hole. Do this for each fish.

6 Cut another length of wool to hang up your mobile. Tie a knot in one end. Thread the wool through the centre hole. Hang your mobile in a window to catch the light and the breeze, and watch it sparkle.

21

Glossary and Index

baked food cooked in an oven

ceremony an event or performance to mark a special occasion

fins parts of the body of a fish that are used to swim and for balance

fry the name given to a newly hatched fish

gills the parts of a fish's body that it uses to breathe

grilled cooked over a fire or under a grill

joints places in the body where two bones meet, for example the elbow, knee and shoulder

nutrients nutrients are found in food. Our bodies need them to grow strong and healthy.

scales small, stiff flakes that cover a fish's body

traditional a custom or way of doing something that is passed from parent to child

vitamins our bodies need these substances in very small amounts for good health

April Fools' Day 18
Atlantic salmon 7

baked food 13, 22
barbel 16

carp 4, 5, 17, 18
catfish 19
caviar 13
ceremony 19, 22
Christmas Eve 18
cod 5, 13, 16
cod-liver oil 14

eggs 4, 8, 13, 16

fins 6, 17, 22
fish farms 5, 9, 10-11, 12, 17
fish fingers 13
fish oil 4, 14-15

food for fish 8, 9, 10
food from fish 4, 12-13, 18, 19
France 18
fry 8, 16, 22

Germany 18
giant catfish 19
gills 6, 22
grilled food 13, 22

halibut 17
hoki 13

joints 14, 22

Koi carp 17

meat 4, 14, 19
mobile 20-1

nutrients 10, 22

oil 4, 14-15
omega-3 15

rainbow trout 5, 15

salmon 5, 7, 11, 12, 14, 15
scales 5, 22
sea bass 5
sturgeon 13

Thailand 19
tilapia 5, 16
traditional customs 18-19, 22
trout 5, 7, 8, 9, 14, 15

vitamins 14, 22

Ideas for teachers and parents

- Visit a fishmonger or a fish market to *see* the range of fish on sale. See if you can find out which fish have come from fish farms and which have been caught in the wild.

- Look for some interesting fish recipes in a cookbook and help the children to make the dish.

- Visit a trout or salmon farm. Many fish farms have open days when members of the public can visit. Open days allow children to *see* all the stages in the life cycle of the fish.

- Make a collage of a fish. Take a large piece of white paper and draw the outline of a fish onto it. Look through old magazines and cut out any pictures of fish and fish-related subjects. Stick these onto the outline to make a colourful fish.

- Visit a public aquarium to *see* all sorts of fish close up.

- Buy a whole trout. See if the children can identify all the different parts of the fish. Look for the nostrils, mouth, eyes, gills and fins. Use a knife to remove some scales and look at them using a magnifying glass. Ask the children how the fish moves through water. Remove the gill cover and look at the red gills underneath. Explain to the children that the gills help the fish to breathe in water.

- Make a wordsearch using the fish-related vocabulary in this book.

- Read about the different types of fish. Make factsheets about them. Find out whether they live in the sea, rivers or lakes, and what they eat.

- Ask the children to think up jokes and stories about fish. See if they can write a poem or a short story about a fish.

Note
• Check that each child does not have any food allergies before eating any fish or making any dishes that contain fish.